Strength
For
Today

Strength for Today

Devotions for Those Who Are Ill

Vincent and Amy Gallagher

Foreword by Robert Hicks

Fleming H. Revell
A Division of Baker Book House Co
Grand Rapids, Michigan 49516

© 1996 by Vincent G. Gallagher and Amy P. Gallagher

Published by Fleming H. Revell
a division of Baker Book House Company
P.O. Box 6287, Grand Rapids, MI 49516-6287

Printed in the United States of America

Library of Congress Cataloging-in-Publication Data

Gallagher, Vincent.
    Strength for today : devotions for those who are ill /
Vincent and Amy Gallagher : foreword by Robert Hicks.
    p.   cm.
  ISBN 0-8007-5583-9 (paper)
  1. Sick—Prayer-books and devotions—English. 2.
Health—Religious aspects—Christianity. I. Gallagher, Amy,
1968–   . II. Title.
BV270.G35   1996
242'.4—dc20   95-44368

Unless otherwise noted, all Scripture is taken from the HOLY BIBLE,
NEW INTERNATIONAL VERSION®. NIV®. Copyright © 1973,
1978, 1984 by International Bible Society. Used by permission of
Zondervan Publishing House. All rights reserved.

Other versions cited are the New King James Version (NKJV), the
New American Standard Bible (NASB), and the King James Version
(KJV).

This book is dedicated to our children:
Catherine Alyssa
John Francis

And to each other

And, to you, the reader

May the grace of the Lord Jesus Christ,
and the love of God,
and the fellowship of the Holy Spirit
be with you all.
2 Corinthians 13:14

Contents

7

Foreword

Whoever thought life is a bed of roses never spent a night in a thorn patch—or lived in my house. Most of the people I know face some kind of pain, problem, or perplexity every day. For the souls of those who have spent more time among the thorns than roses, Vince and Amy Gallagher have penned a healing balm. I have found their husband-and-wife perspectives on pain to be focused on reality, biblically based, and Christ-centered.

Robert Hicks
Chaplain (Lt. Col.), Air National Guard
Author of *Failure to Scream*
and *The Masculine Journey*

Strength

The Lord, the Lord, is my strength
and my song;
he has become my salvation.
Isaiah 12:2

The orderly wheeled Edna into recovery. She had just undergone a surgical procedure. As the anesthesia slowly wore off she opened her eyes briefly, then shut them again.

Edna had walked into the hospital on her own the previous day. She was talkative and appeared strong. Now, lying on the bed, she seemed just the opposite.

"Edna, how do you feel?" I (Amy) asked, holding her I.V.–pierced hand. I squeezed it and awaited her response.

No answer.

"Edna, how do you feel?" I asked louder.

Her eyes opened. Managing a light smile, she said softly, "Weak. I feel weak." Her eyes shut and her hand went limp.

"Lord, please give Edna strength," I prayed softly as I held her limp hand.

God did not abandon Edna in her weakness. As the hours went by, I checked in on her regularly. Finally the color began to return to her face. By the next morning she was sitting up in bed eating her breakfast. She spoke to me.

"I heard you praying, nurse. And you know what? I got my strength back! Now when do I get to leave this hospital? The food stinks!"

I smiled. I silently gave thanks to the Lord who gives strength to the weak.

Dear Lord, I feel weak. Please give me the strength I need physically and emotionally. Be my strength today. Thank you. Amen.

Depression

Why are you downcast, O my soul? . . .
Put your hope in God,
    for I will yet praise him,
    my Savior and my God.

Psalm 42:5

I know about depression.

I (Amy) have suffered several bouts of it during my life. During these times of depression my mood was so low that I just couldn't believe that I would ever feel better. I felt very far from God and unable to reach to him for help. Thanks to God's grace, my depression eventually ended.

I realized that much of it was caused by my own unrealistic expectations of myself. I have learned that God's grace is the real antidote to my bent toward depression. Like many women, I had based my self-worth on my performance in life.

There's a difference between real, disabling depression and the "blues" that everyone occasionally experiences. The severely depressed person honestly believes that his or her life won't improve.

This element of despair is the major symptom of severe depression. The depressed person may also be overly self-critical and have no interest in what he or she used to enjoy. Severe depression may also have a biological component. Physical symptoms may include insomnia and fatigue.

Perhaps you are feeling depressed as you face your illness. Or maybe depression itself is your illness. You are not alone. And if you are willing to ask for help, you will get better.

There is hope. Recovery from depression means making big changes in your life. God is speaking to you through your depression. Can you hear what he is saying? Accepting your limitations, surrendering to his grace, and changing your priorities are key steps to gaining victory.

Ask the Lord to reveal to you the true cause of your depression. You can begin your recovery now by praying this prayer aloud with faith:

Lord, help me to be willing to do the hard work of soul-searching necessary to get better. Help me to understand the truth concerning what my depression is really about. Thank you for your unending faithfulness to me, your child. Amen.

Guidance

I will instruct you and teach you
in the way you should go.
Psalm 32:8

There are so many choices to make when one is diagnosed with a serious illness. Decisions are difficult because they can have far-reaching consequences. Furthermore, these decisions may have to be made when you're on a roller coaster of emotions: First you're scared, then angry, now confused.

How does one make decisions under that kind of pressure? Solomon knew a very important truth. He wrote, "The LORD gives wisdom, and from his mouth come knowledge and understanding" (Prov. 2:6). We must look to Jesus for wisdom and guidance in our decisions. He has promised to give us direction!

The Scripture also says that "many advisers make victory sure" (Prov. 11:14). Have you spoken to several people whom you trust about your options? Here are some guidelines for arriving at a decision.

1. Pray and ask God for guidance and wisdom.
2. Get as much information as you can about all your options.
3. Consult with several people whom you trust.
4. Look at all the pros and cons of each choice.
5. In faith, pick the option that seems best. Take responsibility for your choice and thank God for his guidance.

Then with the psalmist you will be able to say, "You guide me with your counsel" (Ps. 73:24). His guidance and wisdom will surely come to you if you open your heart and mind to his Spirit.

Lord, I have a tough decision to make. Please give me wisdom and guide me to the best decision. Thank you that your Word tells me in James 1:5, "If any of you lacks wisdom, he should ask God, who gives generously to all without finding fault, and it will be given to him." Amen.

Protection

He will cover you with his feathers,
 and under his wings you will find refuge;
 his faithfulness will be your shield
  and rampart.

Psalm 91:4

"I feel so vulnerable! What if something goes wrong? What if the doctor's hand slips? What if the anesthetic hurts me?" anguished Anne, as she sat on the edge of her bed the night before surgery. She looked vulnerable in her skimpy hospital gown.

"Well, we will just have to ask God for protection," I responded.

Perhaps you also are in need of the assurance of God's divine protection. Psalm 91 says, "Because he loves me, I will rescue him; I will protect him, for he acknowledges my name" (v. 14). This precious promise is yours to hold on to. He is able to protect those who turn to him!

Recently we were blessed to be given a home alarm system. If anyone should try to break in, the alarm would sound directly to the local police. I marveled at this wonder of technology that could protect us so efficiently. It made me think of God, who protects the vulnerable.

God doesn't need technology to protect us. He protects us by the power of his Spirit. The same power that raised Christ from the dead is able to protect us in an hour of helplessness.

When three of God's servants were placed in the king's hottest blast furnace, onlookers believed that nothing could protect those men from the fierce flames. Imagine their shock when they realized that the three were not burning up. God's ability to protect his children knew no limits, and his children walked out of the fire without the least harm (Dan. 3:1–30).

After her successful surgery and a brief period of recovery, Anne smiled as she told me, "Everything went fine—I guess God did protect me after all."

Allow the Lord to assure you of his divine protection.

Lord, I ask you for your protection. May your Spirit guide my doctor and protect me from all harm. Amen.

Guilt

But you are a forgiving God, gracious and compassionate, slow to anger and abounding in love.
Nehemiah 9:17

Do you ever feel guilty about being ill?

Being diagnosed with an illness sometimes produces feelings of guilt. Perhaps you feel that your sickness is your fault. Maybe you have, in fact, done things that have led to your becoming ill. You may feel that this illness is punishment for a sin you committed. Seeing the pain and fear that loved ones experience because of your illness may make you feel guilty.

A couple came in to the hospital for some medical testing and there discovered that the wife had lung cancer. At the diagnosis, her husband's face became drawn and pale, and he turned away from her. Although she had stopped smoking two years earlier, she felt tremendous guilt.

You may feel that God is punishing you with your illness but you don't know why. God does not abandon us to our sins and poor choices. We

18

may experience their painful consequences, but in his great mercy he gives us grace to make it through and enables the experience to deepen our reliance on him. We need to lift up our feelings of shame and guilt to the Lord and ask him to forgive us.

By confessing to him in prayer whatever is troubling our conscience, we can rest assured that his forgiveness is complete. We must also ask him to help us to forgive ourselves and take away our guilt.

Dear Lord Jesus, I feel guilty for having this illness and for the pain it causes others. I ask your forgiveness for any sin I have committed. Please help me to walk in your forgiveness and believe that you forgive my sins. Help me to forgive myself. Amen.

Anxiety

I am the LORD, your God,
  who takes hold of your right hand
and says to you, Do not fear;
  I will help you.

Isaiah 41:13

Tom's world changed overnight.

Within twenty-four hours he went from enjoying a family gathering to being on a ventilator in an intensive care unit. He was completely aware of what was happening to him yet was unable to speak because of the tube in his throat. The nursing and medical staff had great difficulty stabilizing his condition. When they gave him sedatives, his vital signs dipped too low. If sedatives were withheld, he was anxious and could not breathe in coordination with the ventilator.

I noticed that Tom's greatest source of anxiety was his inability to communicate. I brought him a pad and pencil. He struggled to write a few words. He indicated that his mouth was dry. I wet his mouth with a cool, moist swab and offered a silent prayer for him. Afterward, he looked visibly relieved and soon dropped off into a deep sleep. The rest of the staff expressed surprise as his breathing and vital signs stabilized without medications.

When we are anxious, our bodies respond to the perceived threat by preparing us to escape from or fight the threat. Our heart races, our muscles tense, our stomach tightens. If the threat is not dealt with, we remain anxious.

Communicating to others exposes our fears and helps decrease our anxiety. We are not alone in facing our trials. The Lord reminds us often in his Word that he is ready and able to calm our anxious minds and remove the threats to our peace and security, and he often places other people in our lives to listen to us.

Tom found peace because he was finally able to communicate with someone about what his needs were. Jesus is waiting for you to express your needs also.

Dear Lord, I feel anxious. I ask you to help me talk with others about my worries. I pray for your peace to fill my mind and body. Amen.

Dependency

For you have been my hope, O Sovereign LORD,
  my confidence since my youth.
From birth I have relied on you.

Psalm 71:5–6

When we are ill we often find that we are no longer able to care for ourselves in the manner we are accustomed to. We may need a ride to the medical facility, or we may need help with our hygiene. Regardless of the situation, having to rely on others can be humbling and may cause us to feel inadequate or frustrated.

Sara was a woman I served whose illness progressed until she was only able to move her head and one finger. This once independent woman had to depend on others to feed and bathe her.

One time, after I had finished bathing her, I overheard her sister ask her how she was coping with being so dependent on others. I will never forget Sara's inspiring reply.

She said, "Most of my life I lived on my own, not relying on anyone but myself. I didn't know God and believed if he did exist I didn't need him either." As her disease progressed she became very angry: "I did not accept what was happening and would not allow others to help. I was soon isolated and afraid; all of my self-reliance didn't amount to anything. The first and most difficult time I ever asked for help was when I asked God to help me. He did."

Sara continued to say that God allowed her to see that he cared for her more completely in his great strength and awesome ability than she had ever cared for herself. "When I saw this, I realized that my dependency on him was good, and it produced a strength I never had," she said. "I may not always like it, but I can finally accept my dependency on others now because it's through my physical dependency that I see how truly dependent I am on him."

Sara found grace in her dependency. My prayer is that you will find grace too.

Lord, relying on others makes me feel scared and frustrated. Please help me to see my dependency on others as a way of reminding me to depend on you. Help me release my burdens into your strong arms and rest in your provision. Thank you, Jesus. Amen.

Fear

Do not fear, for I am with you;
do not be dismayed, for I am your God.
Isaiah 41:10

What is your worst fear? Getting a dreaded disease? Death? Losing someone beloved?

I suffered with a fear that seemed more terrible to me than all of these things: that I would be eternally separated from God.

One night I had a nightmare about being separated from God. The dream seemed so real. When I awoke I caught my breath and tried to bring myself back to reality. I started praying for comfort and as I was praying, I thought of being separated from God. I began to calm down as I realized that God will never abandon those who put their hope in Christ. Jesus experienced separation from God so that we who believe in him might have the assurance of eternal fellowship with our loving heavenly Father.

Fear is destructive because it can overwhelm and paralyze us. As believers we must fight fear because we know that fear is not of God. The Scripture tells us that "God has not given us a spirit of fear" (2 Tim. 1:7 NKJV). My pastor once told me that if we can become a little angry about what we are afraid of it will help us conquer the fear. The best antidote to fear is trusting God and the truth of his Word.

Maybe you have been afraid of something recently. Our God is a God of love and compassion who will not leave you to your fears. The God who provided the answer to life's ultimate fear can provide for you in your current situation. Despite your sins, the Creator of all things loves you enough to promise you that no fear is bigger than his ability to ease it. May you be encouraged that his perfect love will cast out your present fears.

Lord, the fear I am experiencing is sometimes overwhelming. Help me remember that you always provide a way through my fears and are with me in them. Comfort me when I am afraid. In Jesus' name. Amen.

Simplicity

> But I am afraid, lest . . . your minds should be
> led astray from the simplicity and purity of
> devotion to Christ.
>
> 2 Corinthians 11:3 NASB

The stress was really getting to me. I (Vincent) was driving myself to do more and more. At work I was attempting to reform hardened drug users. After some initial success I became completely engrossed with helping them. Yet many were very resistant to my efforts.

Then, looking in the mirror one day, I noticed that one side of my face seemed dead. It was paralyzed. When I smiled, only the other side of my face worked. I couldn't move my eyebrow or one side of my mouth. And I had had an ongoing severe headache.

The doctor diagnosed this strange condition as Bell's palsy. It hit without warning and persisted week after week. I felt humiliated because I was due to begin working at a well-known Christian counseling center and I thought, *Who would want a counselor with a deformed face?*

The Lord had gotten my attention through this illness. He seemed to be telling me to slow down. I felt his Spirit calling me to reexamine my priorities and to simplify my life. He used the illness to show me how driven I really was.

I decided I would leave the stressful drug rehabilitation center. I would simplify my life by moving by faith into a less stressful counseling situation. There was no guarantee I'd be successful, yet I knew that it was the wise thing to do. That was five years ago, and the Lord has confirmed my decision many times over.

Perhaps your illness is causing you to reexamine your life. What is the Holy Spirit saying to you in your illness? I pray that you may hear his voice and obey it.

Lord, please help me to listen. I can't seem to slow down and "smell the roses" on my own. Help me not to strive when I should be resting in you! Please help me to simplify my life and listen to your Spirit. Amen.

Grace

From the fullness of his grace we have all received.

John 1:16

Have you experienced the grace of God?

God loves his children. Nothing can ever separate us from his love. Our sins are forgiven, and God views us with total acceptance. This fact has been accomplished by Jesus' sacrifice on the cross. All we have to do to experience this favor with God is to accept it by faith and confess with our mouths that Jesus Christ is our Lord and Savior. The Scripture assures us that those who are in Christ have received forgiveness of all their sins and possess eternal life with God. That's God's grace.

The human love we have experienced is only a faint glimmer of the glorious love of the Father. He loves us as no one else can—unconditionally and without reserve. All other religions in the world focus on how humanity can reach up to appease heaven. Christianity alone teaches what the Father has done to reach down to humanity. Through his Son, Jesus, God has shared with his people his eternal Spirit. As the apostle Paul tells us, "He who unites himself with the Lord is one with him in spirit" (1 Cor. 6:17).

We must not let our feelings separate us from the assurance of this great love. This simple truth of God's grace can be obscured by our emotions during an illness. Are you feeling doubtful? Feeling like he may be punishing you? Remember God's grace in giving you his unconditional love.

Dear Jesus, thank you for forgiving me of all my sins. Thank you that your unconditional love flows to all your children. Help me to believe that you really do love me, and forgive me when I doubt your grace. Amen.

Pain

Our present sufferings are not worth comparing with the glory that will be revealed in us.
Romans 8:18

I hate pain.

While my wife was giving birth to Catherine, our first child, she was offered some pain relief by the kind maternity nurse. Amy refused, preferring natural childbirth. However, I turned to the nurse and said, "She won't take any, but I will!"

We all laughed, but I wasn't kidding. Just seeing Amy in pain made me want relief for myself!

Most of us hate pain. But like Amy's labor, some pains have a purpose. Sometimes suffering does something to us that nothing else ever could. It is often through pain that we are humbled and turn afresh to God.

The Scripture tells us that even Jesus learned obedience by what he suffered. His pain was used by God to help him yield to the will of the Father.

Similarly, our pain can be used by God, mysteriously, to refine, purge, and renew our spirit.

As a professor at a Christian college, I get the opportunity to challenge my students to think critically. I recently asked them this question: What is the surest route to spiritual maturity if we allow it to do its work in us? Some said Scripture memorization, others, church attendance, and still others, commitment and obedience. I assured them these are all good routes, but one way stands out above all others: suffering—or rather, our reaction to suffering. We can allow pain to make us bitter and cynical or we can allow it to break us and turn us to Jesus. The choice is always ours.

No pain is meaningless for a Christian.

Dear Jesus, help me in my pain. Help me not to despair in my pain but to realize that I am sharing in your sufferings. Please conform me into what you'd have me become. Amen.

Sleep

For he grants sleep to those he loves.
Psalm 127:2

The hospital chapel was full. Patients and families sat still during the hour-long Sunday service. During the sermon I talked about the great love of Jesus. Afterward Amy and I stayed to pray for those who requested prayer.

A young patient was wheeled toward us by his mother. He had been injured in an auto accident. "Please pray that I can get some sleep at night. The lack of sleep is driving me crazy!" he explained.

We prayed.

The next week, he was wheeled forward again. "Praise the Lord!" he beamed. "After prayer last week I slept soundly that night for the first time in a long while! As a matter of fact I've slept great all week long!"

Sleep. We can take it for granted when we experience it regularly. But for those who are ill, restless nights are commonplace. And lack of sleep can hinder the body's ability to recover from illness.

Sleep deprivation causes us to become irritable and anxious. We become more sensitive to pain. Depression can result. Concentration and decision making are negatively affected.

The Scripture tells us that God gives sleep to his beloved. What a wonderful promise! Perhaps you are having difficulty getting a good night's sleep. Turn to Jesus and ask him for the gift of sleep.

Dear Lord, I feel exhausted! Please allow me to sleep undisturbed. Send your angels to protect me and bring sweet slumber. Thank you that your Word promises that you give sleep to your beloved. Amen.

A Glimpse of Heaven

I know a man in Christ who . . . was caught up to . . . heaven.

2 Corinthians 12:2

I was always afraid of death. When I was a young man, several of my closest friends were accidentally killed. Afterward I was terrorized by nightmares in which these friends appeared and taunted me in a devilish manner. These nightmares continued for years.

Even after my conversion to Christ I felt a sense of terror about death. Even though I knew intellectually that believers need not fear death, I was bound by uncontrollable feelings of horror whenever I was exposed to it. My grandfather and other relatives and friends died as the years went by, and the nightmares intensified whenever I had to attend a viewing or a funeral.

Then a miracle occurred for me.

My cousin, a young woman in her early thirties, died unexpectedly. That night as I slept I dreamed a dream that seemed as real as my waking life. My cousin and my grandfather, both believers in Christ, were with me in a church. They were radiantly healthy and bathed in light. They told me of their wonderful existence. It felt so good to be with them, surrounded in their love and joy, that I didn't want to leave. When I awoke, my room was filled with the peaceful presence of the Holy Spirit. I felt as if I'd been given a glimpse of heaven.

My fear of death has never returned.

Dear Jesus, sometimes I'm afraid when I contemplate death. Help me catch a glimpse of heaven, and fill me with your perfect love. Amen.

Making Amends

Forgive your brother from your heart.
Matthew 18:35

Jack had experienced years of bad relationships with his family. As he lay ill on his hospital bed, he was forced to examine his life. He turned to God in prayer.

Afterward he began to get a sense that he needed to forgive some specific people and ask to be forgiven as well. He promised God that he would make amends to those he had hurt and determined also to forgive those who had offended him.

As his family came to visit him, some came not out of love but out of duty. One day his brother Ted walked into the hospital room and Jack saw his opportunity.

"Ted, come closer," Jack said, hoarsely.

Ted looked a bit uneasy. He walked slowly over

to the bedside. It was difficult for him to be there. He'd been harboring resentment toward Jack for years. Seeing Jack so ill made him feel guilty. He wanted to leave.

"Ted, let me have your hand," Jack said.

His brother hesitated and then held it out, warily.

Jack grasped his brother's hand, and his tears began to flow.

"Ted, I'm sorry for all the pain I may have caused you through the years. I really am sorry. Can you ever forgive me?" Jack asked, tears streaming down his face.

The other family members in the room wept as they saw Ted bend over the bed and embrace his brother for the first time in thirty years.

Although Jack's body was still sick, his soul was being healed, and he was healing the soul of his family as well.

Is there someone you need to forgive? Do it now.

Dear Jesus, help me to forgive those who have hurt me, and give me the humility to ask forgiveness from those I've offended. Amen.

Hurry Up
and Wait

Be still before the LORD and wait patiently for
   him.

Psalm 37:7

I hate to wait!

Illness is a time of waiting. We wait for the
doctor, the nurse, the treatment, and the lab
results. As a nurse I have seen many responses
to waiting. Usually these responses include frustration, impatience, and restlessness!

One particularly hectic morning I spied an
older woman waiting in our overcrowded waiting area, so I asked her if I could help. She told
me that she had been waiting for more than two
hours to have some blood tests. I realized that
she had not signed in and so was still not in line
to be seen. I was concerned for her, but she did
not appear to be bothered in the least.

She told me, "On any other day I might have

been really angry. But something happened to me today! If I had been seen in turn when I arrived, I would have missed a blessing from God! Because I had to wait, I ended up sitting next to a woman who had the same illness I have. We talked and exchanged phone numbers. I have been asking God to give me someone who understands what I am going through, and he did. No, I did not mind waiting today and I don't think I ever will again!"

The Lord spoke to me through that woman. Waiting gives us opportunities, if we can be made aware of them—opportunities to rest, to reach out to others, to exercise our faith, to pray or read his Word. Let us ask the Lord to show us how to use the time we spend waiting.

Heavenly Father, it is difficult for me to wait, especially when it is for information about my health. Show me how you would have me wait and give me the patience to do so. Thank you, Lord. Amen.

Ministers of God

In the day of my trouble I will call to you.
Psalm 86:7

I (Vincent) was very ill. My fever ran to 105 degrees. My body was racked with aches; every move hurt. My head pounded, my stomach was churning, and my throat was swollen with infection. I hadn't been out of bed for three days. I was miserable.

I was lying on my back in bed, tossing to and fro, unable to sleep, depressed and despairing when suddenly the door of my bedroom swung open.

My friend Mike walked in. His smile broke through my gloom. "I'm here to pray for you, brother!" he announced.

Mike's hand was on my head. "Dear Jesus, please heal my brother. May your Spirit renew him and fill him with your healing and your

40

peace. Protect him against the evil one, and raise him up!"

The room was filled with a spirit of hope. The light of Jesus dispelled the darkness of my body and soul.

I tried to express my appreciation to my friend.

"Jesus will heal you, brother," he responded. "I love you. Just try to rest." With that, he was gone. The whole visit lasted only ten minutes. That night my fever finally broke.

Perhaps today will be the day that your ministering spirit comes.

Dear Lord, thank you for the ministering spirits you send our way. Help me to recognize your love and care through the servants you use to minister to me. Amen.

God's Promise

Do not be afraid; do not be discouraged . . . the LORD will be with you.

2 Chronicles 20:17

My grandfather was born in 1896. When he was in his eighties I asked him, "What have you learned in all your long years of life?" He looked at me with his aged eyes and said, "I've learned not to worry. It seems to me that I spent my whole life worrying about things that never happened after all."

Worry. It's something we all experience occasionally. But when we're ill worry can consume us. *Will I lose something I'll never get back?* we wonder. *What if everything doesn't work out all right?* These questions can torment us, causing the thoughts in our minds to become that horrible feeling of dread in our stomachs.

Jesus will help the believer through the fires of

trials. Although we may go through pain, it will not ultimately beat us. The pain will stop, and his victory will be ours. Even Jesus himself did not stay suffering on the cross forever, but for a specific period of time. And then his resurrection occurred, and the pain was banished for eternity!

God does not promise to keep us from encountering difficulties in this life. His promise to us is that the trials will not overtake us and that he will give us strength to weather the storm.

And our worst fears usually never materialize.

Lord, help us to know that we never need to worry, because your love will bring us through any trial that comes our way. Thank you for your promise that you will always be with me. Amen.

Tender Mercies

Do not withhold your mercy from me, O LORD.
Psalm 40:11

The little things. Isn't that what life is really comprised of? The little joys—like a child's sweet laughter or a smile from someone who loves you. Or a good meal! The list may be endless. Although we all dream of "big" events that will make us happy, like a wedding, graduation, or retirement, it is really the small things that make up our lives.

I (Amy) call them God's tender mercies.

What are the little things that brighten your day? Can you think of some?

When we are ill, food loses its taste. People irritate us. The things that previously brought us pleasure only leave us uninspired. We may be so focused on what's wrong that we forget to count our blessings.

44

Our God is a God of mercy. As we wait on him, he will surely lift the blanket of discouragement from us. We will enjoy life again as we see his tender mercies toward us.

See the care of the heavenly Father in those who care for you. A nurse, doctor, minister, or loved one may not look like an angel, but in each person's own way, he or she is a reflection of God's love.

Lord, help me to appreciate the little things in my life and see them as a reflection of your love and care. Amen.

Away from Home

In my Father's house are many rooms . . . I am going there to prepare a place for you.

John 14:2

Most people suffer feelings of homesickness when they stay in the hospital. Many hospitals and nursing centers attempt to achieve a home-like atmosphere in their facilities by adding colorful wallpaper and decorations. But as nice as they try to make it, there's just no place like home.

While in the hospital we have to depend on others to provide for most of our needs. We often have to share a room with a complete stranger at a time in our lives when we need the most privacy. The smells are unusual and the noises and routines unfamiliar. Home seems like the warmest and safest of havens when we are in the hospital!

But there is another home that we often don't

think of in our daily lives—our heavenly Father's home. Paul tells us that we are only travelers in this world, pilgrims on a journey to our ultimate home with God.

Our heavenly home has been prepared for us by Jesus in anticipation of our coming. There will be no stress or illness in our heavenly home, only peace and love with Jesus and our loved ones in him. We will have no more pain, no more tears, and no more disappointment. Our true home awaits us as a place of refuge and safety forever.

Regardless of whether your discharge from the hospital is days or weeks away, you need to ask the Lord to help you remember that your earthly home is only a temporary place for you, that in your heart you are seated "with him in the heavenly realms" (Eph. 2:6).

There truly is no place like home.

Dear Jesus, I miss being home where it is familiar and safe. Please help me to be patient while I heal and help me to remember that my true home is with you. Help me feel your security and take refuge in your arms. Amen.

Appearances

Though outwardly we are wasting away, yet
inwardly we are being renewed day by day.
2 Corinthians 4:16

"What will I look like after this procedure is
over?" asked Anita as she pondered the impact
of her surgery. Hers is a common concern for
many going through surgery, cancer treatment,
or chronic illness. Changes in our appearance can
make us feel old, unattractive, or different from
others.

In our society a person's self-image is too often
based on his or her physical attributes. As a nurse
I have observed many surgeries and have
thought, once you get past the very thin layer of
skin, we all look the same! Beauty is truly only
skin deep.

Once I was reading the story of Snow White
to my daughter, Catherine. We got to the sec-
tion where the wicked witch asked the magic mirror, "Who is the fairest of them all?"

My three-year-old turned to me and said with a giggle, "Jesus is the fairest one of all!"

How simple, yet true. Christ within us is where our beauty lies. For the believer, real beauty is in the heart, not the flesh.

Are you feeling scarred or unattractive? Just remember that you are beautiful in Jesus. Real beauty is a heart filled with Christ and his love. The beauty of the flesh must fade in everyone. But the beauty of a believer in Christ continues forever.

Dear Jesus, thank you for this body that you have given me, with its strengths as well as its frailties. Help me adapt to the changes in my body and help me see myself the way you do, as a beautiful, unique child. Thank you, Jesus. Amen.

Weakness

For when I am weak, then I am strong.
2 Corinthians 12:10

Have you ever seen the commercials on television advertising exercise equipment? The makers claim that for a small investment you can change your life. Your weak body will be transformed into a muscular powerhouse. The message is clear: Weakness is bad; strength is good.

God has a different message.

When the apostle Paul experienced feelings of weakness, he pleaded, "Take this thorn away from me." For Paul the burden of the thorn was unbearable.

We are used to being strong. When we are ill we become weak. This is seldom easy, so we instinctively cry out as Paul did, "Take this burden away, Lord!"

Sometimes he does. But in the mystery of his

will, sometimes he doesn't. Then we have to listen to the reply he gave the apostle: "My grace is sufficient for you, for my power is made perfect in weakness" (2 Cor. 12:9).

What does this verse mean? It means that we need to pray for God's strength. It means we need to trust that he will give us the grace we need to face our illness. It means that he is always faithful to us, even in the midst of pain.

God's message is clear.

Dear Lord, I feel so weak and helpless. Help me accept my weakness that I might receive your strength. Amen.

One Day at a Time

> Do not worry about tomorrow, for tomorrow will worry about itself.
>
> Matthew 6:34

Jesus tells us to take life one day at a time.

When we are ill we may begin to dread the future. We allow ourselves to think the worst: *What if I don't recover fully?* Dread begins to fill our mind. We think about the effect of our illness on loved ones. We wonder who will pay the bills. We fear the pain. We often fear consequences that might take place six months or more into the future!

But Jesus tells us not to be anxious about tomorrow. He reminds us that his grace is with us as we live one day at a time.

God was faithful to feed the Israelites in the wilderness. The manna came down from heaven every day. But when God's people began to hoard the food against an uncertain future, the manna rotted.

It is the same with us: His grace is good, one day at a time. Tomorrow he will be as faithful as he is today, so we needn't fear.

One way I (Amy) help Christian patients see things in perspective concerning their fears is to remind them of God's past faithfulness.

Bertha was an elderly woman facing the prospect of moving out of her home of forty years and living in a long-term care facility. She was full of fear about what tomorrow might bring. I'll never forget how her eyes finally sparkled after a time of prayer I had with her. She looked up at me and said, "Ain't nothin' gonna happen to me today that the Lord can't handle." Bertha learned the secret of living one day at a time.

Dear Lord, please help me live life one day at a time and not worry about tomorrow. Remind me of your mercies in the past so I can trust you with my future. Thank you, Jesus. Amen.

Trust

The LORD is good. . . .
He cares for those who trust in him.
Nahum 1:7

Did you ever play the childhood game of falling backward into the arms of another child? I (Vincent) used to play that game. But I would only go through with it if I was sure the other person would really catch me. Frankly, I refused to fall on some people! Yet with others I'd do it in a minute, unhesitatingly. I knew whom I could trust and whom I couldn't.

Trust is something lots of religious people talk about. But when we're ill trust in God is tested. "What side effects will this medicine produce?" "When will I get better?" "What if I get worse?" we ask. We know in our head we can trust God, but in our heart—well, that's a bit harder.

The best way to build trust with someone is to know him or her well. Years of a relationship can produce an unshakable bond of trust. It's the same way with God. The longer we know him, the more we realize his trustworthiness. And unlike a person, God is perfectly trustworthy.

Are you struggling with trust? Do you want to rest in his perfect peace, knowing that he is trustworthy? Jeremiah tells us:

> Blessed is the man who trusts in the LORD,
>   whose confidence is in him.
> He will be like a tree planted by the water
>   that sends out its roots by the stream.
> It does not fear when heat comes;
>   its leaves are always green.
> It has no worries in a year of drought
>   and never fails to bear fruit.
>
> Jeremiah 17:7–8

Dear Jesus, please help me trust you during this trial. Allow me to feel your caring presence with me. Help me know that nothing can happen to me that you can't take care of. I want to trust you and I put my life in your hands. Amen.

Rest

There remains, then, a Sabbath-rest for the people of God.

Hebrews 4:9

Recently I (Vincent) was sitting on the couch watching television. Our three-year-old daughter, Catherine, was stretched out on the couch with her head on a pillow in my lap. As I watched the show I gently stroked her soft blond hair. She rested there and soon she was asleep. Her little face, with her eyes closed in perfect peace, was the picture of rest. Looking at her I realized that the Father desires us to rest also.

There comes a time when we must surrender our efforts to God and cease our striving. For most of us, this is difficult!

When we are ill we learn what we must do to help our healing. It might be changing our diet or exercising. There is usually something we can do to promote our recovery.

But sometimes, when the illness is severe, we run out of treatment options. It is at these times that the Lord calls us to rest in him in a special way.

It may seem impossible to rest after a lifetime of striving. We are part of a society that thrives on activity and busyness, rendering physical rest difficult. Our minds are filled with thoughts; we may feel powerless—after all, there must be something we can do, some angle we can figure out. Mental rest then is difficult.

The Bible tells us that God rested after working hard. The Book of Hebrews tells us that there is this same "Sabbath-rest" for his people. He will enable us to rest if we will open our hearts to him.

Are you restless? Do you long to rest like a child in God's loving arms?

Dear Jesus, help me to rest in your presence and cease from my striving and worry. Amen.

Healing

For he had healed many, so that those with diseases were pushing forward to touch him.

Mark 3:10

A man who had been ill for many years had
given up hope. He was no longer able to get himself up and seek help. But his friends had great
faith and they carried him to the Healer.

Jesus was teaching in a home crowded with
people. Suddenly, the roof above their heads
opened, and down came a sick man on a bed.
Jesus spoke to the man, assuring him that his
sins were forgiven. And then he touched him.
The man was healed! Imagine the excitement!

Many of us hope for healing when we are ill.
The Bible encourages us to have the persevering
prayer of a woman who needed help. She kept
on asking and eventually she received her
request. We should keep asking God to heal us.

Sometimes it helps our faith when we realize
that God has healed us in the past. Look back
into your own life. You will see, through the eyes

of faith, that God has helped you through every problem. How many times has he used medicine, doctors, nurses, prayer, and direct aid to heal your illnesses? It may be easy to forget how often he has ministered to you. The psalmist writes that God heals all of your diseases (Ps. 103:3). You must not lose heart, but keep praying. Ask others to pray for you too.

Jesus is the great healer. He will answer you in his time and in his way. He will always respond to the needs of his children. Perhaps you have become discouraged in prayer. Don't stop praying for healing. The answer is already on the way!

Dear Lord, please heal me. Help me not to become discouraged. Give me the grace to wait for your perfect timing. Amen.

Our Breath

The LORD God formed the man from the dust
of the ground and breathed into his nostrils
the breath of life, and the man became a living
being.

Genesis 2:7

Our bodies carry the miracle of the "breath
of life" the Scripture speaks of. Very few of us
ever notice our breathing because it is such a
natural aspect of our living. We tend to take it
for granted.

Yet if you have ever been deprived of oxygen,
you probably have experienced panic. Then you
realized that life is indeed dependent on the flow
of air through your lungs. When that flow is
threatened, survival is at stake.

For those with respiratory ailments the simple
act of breathing becomes a very serious matter.
They may have to cope with feelings of alarm on
a routine basis. Their mobility is often impaired
because of the reduced amount of oxygen available to their muscle cells.

Breathing in fills our lungs with oxygen to be used for every body function. Breathing out rids our bodies of wastes. Breathing regularly keeps our systems in balance.

It is significant that the Holy Spirit is likened to breath. When Jesus sent out the apostles, "he breathed on them and said, 'Receive the Holy Spirit'" (John 20:22). Jesus breathed new life into the apostles that sounded "like the blowing of a violent wind" (Acts 2:2) at Pentecost. Jesus himself told Nicodemus that everyone born of the Holy Spirit is like the wind blowing (John 3:8).

Before this filling of the Holy Spirit, people were hindered from serving God in the fullness of spiritual vitality. But the filling of the Holy Spirit enables the body of Christ—the church—to come alive in divine power. God's Spirit empowers us to carry out his purpose in our lives.

Perhaps you need to be renewed in the Holy Spirit today. Pray this prayer and anticipate God's response by faith.

Dear Jesus, please fill me afresh with your Holy Spirit. Fill me up with your presence and anoint me with a renewal of your Spirit. Thank you for this breath of eternal life. Amen.

Relaxation

He got up, rebuked the wind and said to the waves, "Quiet! Be still!" Then the wind died down and it was completely calm.

Mark 4:39

At different points in our lives it becomes necessary to find time to relax and have the stormy seas of our lives calmed. Illness can provide us with more unscheduled time. However, many of us do not know how to rebuke the wind and the waves and use the time to relax. We have many concerns on our mind.

As a nurse I have taught people slow deep-breathing techniques that help them quiet themselves. These techniques have been employed by people who are anxious, experiencing pain, or recovering from surgery. They are also used for natural childbirth or in managing chronic illness.

I have even taught my daughter to use this breathing when she feels overwhelmed. Here is one technique. Read through it once and then practice it yourself.

You can do this exercise sitting, standing, or lying down. Close your eyes and breathe normally a few times. Now take a slow, deep breath in through your nose. Hold it for one to two seconds. Just as slowly, release your breath through your mouth. As you exhale, imagine the air flowing down your arms and legs, exiting through your fingertips and toes. Repeat with another slow, deep breath. Allow the Lord's peace to reach all of your cells.

This simple breathing exercise accomplishes several things. Physically, it expands your lungs more fully, allowing you to take in more oxygen. It enables more waste products to be exhaled. Then your pulse slows down. Your muscles release their tension. Mentally, slow and deep breathing gives you something concrete to focus on. It helps you feel more in control. Then your thoughts don't race. Spiritually, you are quieted enough to pray, unhampered by anxious feelings and scrambled thoughts.

You can receive Christ's peace into your body. Begin by asking the Lord to help you relax. Allow him to rebuke your storms and calm you.

Dear Lord, I have many things on my mind and I can't be still and relax. Help me accept the peace you have for me. Please quiet my mind, body, and spirit. Thank you, Jesus. Amen.

Serenity

And the peace of God, which transcends all understanding, will guard your hearts and your minds in Christ Jesus.

Philippians 4:7

In the 1950s Reinhold Niebuhr wrote a prayer that has become famous. It begins like this: "God, grant me the serenity to accept the things I cannot change, the courage to change the things I can, and the wisdom to know the difference." Like most simple prayers, it is really quite profound.

First, it acknowledges that all inner peace and serenity can only come from God. It is not determined by our circumstances, but rather it is a work of grace in our hearts. This grace gives us the ability to truly accept things that we have no control over.

Second, the prayer shows that there are things over which we do have control. It is these things that must be identified and then acted upon. Too often we experience the reverse of this prayer; we don't accept the things we have no control over, and what we can change we fail to.

Third, the prayer acknowledges that only God can give us the wisdom to know the difference. It truly is a wonderful prayer, which can lead us to a deeper level of God's peace.

Are there things in your life right now that you have no control over? Ask Jesus to help you accept these things.

And what about the things that you can change? Do you know what these things are? Ask him to show you and give you the courage to change them.

Inner peace and serenity do not come cheaply or easily. By his death on the cross, Jesus has given believers peace with God. Ask him to help you experience this inner peace and serenity in all the other areas of your life as well.

God, grant me the serenity to accept the things I cannot change, the courage to change the things I can, and the wisdom to know the difference. Amen.

Renewing Our Minds

Do not conform any longer to the pattern of this world, but be transformed by the renewing of your mind.

Romans 12:2

Assaults on our self-esteem can seem constant. It is difficult to go through a day and not experience some of their effects. Our culture tells us how we should act, think, and look to be acceptable.

As Christians our desire is to be like Jesus, not like the world. We must train our mind to think as he does and to see life from his eternal perspective instead of our temporal one.

Worldly misconceptions that distort our thinking must be brought before the truth of his Word. Here are some thoughts common to many of us and what God has to say about them.

Thought	God's Response
I am so ugly.	No! "He has made everything beautiful in its time" (Eccles. 3:11). You are beautiful in his sight!

Thought	God's Response
I am all alone in this.	No! "And surely I am with you always, to the very end of the age" (Matt. 28:20). He is with you!
There is nothing special about me.	No! "But you are a chosen people, a royal priesthood, a holy nation, a people belonging to God" (1 Peter 2:9). You are holy and precious to him—his royal child!
I feel like the only one who has ever had this problem.	No! "For we do not have a high priest who is unable to sympathize with our weaknesses, but we have one who has been tempted in every way, just as we are—yet was without sin" (Heb. 4:15). He struggled with what you are going through and he will help you overcome!
No one knows the real me.	No! "Before I formed you in the womb I knew you, before you were born I set you apart" (Jer. 1:5). He made you; he knows you; he loves you!

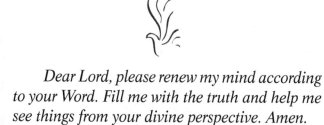

Dear Lord, please renew my mind according to your Word. Fill me with the truth and help me see things from your divine perspective. Amen.

Poor in Spirit

Blessed are the poor in spirit,
  for theirs is the kingdom of heaven.
                    Matthew 5:3

I (Amy) had no more answers. I had run out of prayers. I had read all the Scriptures that I could and they had left me empty and dry. My faith had hit bottom; I was inconsolable and full of doubts.

I had been raised in a Christian home and had always believed in God's provision and presence in my life. Then, in the midst of the most serious crisis of my life, I felt let down by all the tools of faith that I had used since childhood. Prayer, Bible study, church attendance—they all left me unmoved. I felt empty, spiritually impoverished.

In the Amplified version of the Bible, Matthew 5:3 reads, "Blessed—happy, to be envied, and spiritually prosperous—are the poor in spirit."

Why are the poor in spirit to be envied? How could they be described as spiritually prosperous? That is certainly not how I had seen myself during my spiritual low.

Jesus knew that only when we are emptied of our efforts and striving can we be filled with his Spirit. In that state we can truly allow his strength to work in our lives. All our religiosity will fail us; in our spiritual poverty we are blessed because then the stage is set for the manifestation of God's love.

During my crisis I came to the place where all I could pray was, "Lord, I need you. Please help me." I came to accept my spiritual poverty and in doing so was able to receive the grace I needed to go forward. Jesus showed me that my efforts had actually blocked my ability to receive help from him. He taught me the true extent of my spiritual poverty and led me to the riches of his love.

Dear Lord, take my impoverished spirit and fill me with the riches of your self. I give up all my self-effort and surrender to you. Amen.

Faith or Fear?

Do not be afraid or discouraged because of this vast army. For the battle is not yours, but God's.
2 Chronicles 20:15

The good King Jehoshaphat was afraid. He was outnumbered. From a human standpoint, the odds were totally against him. The armies of many nations were on their way to attack his smaller force. So he did the only thing he could under the circumstances: He turned to the Lord for help.

Jehoshaphat prayed, "O our God, will you not judge them? For we have no power to face this vast army that is attacking us. We do not know what to do, but our eyes are upon you" (2 Chron. 20:12).

King Jehoshaphat acknowledged that his strength was insufficient for the task. He knew he needed the help that only God could bring.

The Lord spoke through a messenger and told the king, "You will not have to fight this battle. Take up your positions; stand firm and see the deliverance the LORD will give you" (v. 17). The armies were still closing in. The problem was still very real. Yet God encouraged Jehoshaphat to trust. And then, God acted with power! When the Israelites began to sing and praise the Lord from their positions, the Lord "set ambushes" against the attacking armies (v. 22). The invaders began to fight each other. All the enemy armies were utterly destroyed.

Like Jehoshaphat, you may also feel overwhelmed with impossible situations. Maybe you see your circumstances and are afraid. You know that there is no human answer to the problem you are facing. Ask the Lord to help you turn to him in your time of need, as did King Jehoshaphat. May you be encouraged until your faith becomes sight and the Lord conquers all of your enemies, whether they are sickness, disease, or even death itself.

Dear Lord, the problem seems so big, but you are bigger still. Help me to stand and see you fight for me. Take away my fear and replace it with faith. Amen.

God Is in Control

In all things God works for the good of those who love him.

Romans 8:28

Imagine the degradation of being a slave. What could be more humiliating than being sold to someone else?

Joseph not only was sold into slavery but also was betrayed by his own family. Yet God was faithful to him and eventually freed him. Joseph eventually was in the position to save his people from starvation. Although Satan meant to bring evil through it, God brought good from it.

It may be hard to see how God could use your painful illness for good. Still his Word assures you that this is so. He promises to use all your experiences to draw you closer to him. He is truly in control, even when you feel overcome by evil.

When I (Vincent) look back on my life I can

see how God used each of my illnesses to teach me something, whether it was the need to reexamine my life or to rest. I may not have liked the lessons or even been aware of their benefit or of God's hand at the time, but in retrospect, I can see that God was in control.

Perhaps you are having difficulty seeing how God could bring anything good out of your illness. His Word promises that there is a reason for all things, and you must trust in the mystery of his will.

Lord, help me see your hand at work in the midst of this bad thing that is happening to me. Help me trust you to bring good out of it. Amen.

Miracles

The apostles performed many miraculous signs and wonders among the people.

Acts 5:12

Christians believe in miracles. Our entire faith rests on the miraculous. The revelation of God came through miracles. The virgin birth, the healings of Jesus, the resurrection from the dead—God showed his love and power toward us through all these miraculous events.

We must never stop believing in the miracles of the Lord Jesus. During the last fifteen years I (Vincent) have seen dozens of healing miracles. One, in particular, stands out.

Amy began to complain of a sharp pain in her side. I was a seminary student, and our health insurance was minimal. Amy went to the doctor, who diagnosed an ovarian cyst. It was hoped that hormonal pills would make surgery unnecessary.

As I prayed over Amy for healing, I began to hear the words *bitterness* and *unforgiveness* in my mind. I asked her about these words, and we then discerned that the cyst had some emotional cause. Amy began to cry and confessed that she was indeed hurt and angry with one of her parents. As I led her through a prayer of forgiveness, she fell into a deep sleep. She slept uninterrupted for eleven hours.

On awakening, she realized that the pain was gone. She went to the doctor, and he declared that her cyst had vanished. She had received a healing miracle from Jesus.

We must never despair of God's intervention in our lives. Perhaps you need a miracle today. Ask God for it. Ask a believing friend to pray for you. Go ahead and ask your chaplain, minister, or priest to anoint you with oil for healing, as the Bible tells us to do in James 5:14.

Miracles still happen.

Dear Lord, I ask for a miracle. Please heal me of my condition and strengthen me to serve you. Amen.

Reaching Out to Others

Give, and it will be given to you.
Luke 6:38

I had a broken heart. A relationship had ended, and I (Vincent) was still feeling deeply hurt. I was a student at Eastern College and I began avoiding a particular dormitory because of the pain associated with it. My former girlfriend had lived there, and whenever I even looked at the brick building my heart ached.

One night after a meeting of the fellowship I led, a girl who had attended asked me to escort her back to her dorm. As we walked out of the chapel into the cold autumn air I was surprised that she headed toward the building I had been avoiding. I thought she lived on the opposite side of the campus. As we walked closer to the dormitory I felt the hurtful memories flood my mind and I began to grieve. I couldn't bear to go any closer and asked the girl if I could stand and watch until she got to the door safely. Instead of agreeing, she asked me to come inside and pray for her about a physical ailment. I couldn't refuse.

As I stood in the student lounge, the very place where I had been so badly hurt, the girl asked me to pray for her heart. She had a ventricular problem.

Praying for Jesus to heal her heart, I suddenly heard him say to me, *Since you ask for her heart to be healed, I will heal your own heart.* Suddenly I felt the presence of the Holy Spirit all around me. As I left that night I realized I no longer felt the oppressive weight I had previously experienced.

When we step out of ourselves and help others, often we find that we receive much more than we give.

Dear Lord, help me to get my mind off my own problems and help others, even in the midst of my pain. Amen.

Asking for Help

He will deliver the needy who cry out,
the afflicted who have no one to help.
Psalm 72:12

I used to try to be a superwoman. I felt that I should never ask for help and that I should somehow know how to do all things. Irrational, but true.

As a new nurse I quickly realized that unless I accepted my limitations and asked for help, I could never grow to maturity. It was very humbling for me to admit to myself and others that I could not do it all.

I have nursed many people who lost their ability to care for themselves. I have noticed that those who accept their limitations and ask for help have more inner peace in their lives. Those who do not, suffer frustration.

In a world where independence and self-reliance

are highly valued, it can be humbling to need the help of others. Asking for help requires acknowledging our neediness. And many of us are ashamed of being needy.

Jesus encourages us in the Scriptures to ask for help. He reminds us that the Father wants to help us, if only we will ask.

Indeed, he knows our needs even before we ask. We must remember to ask for what we need first from him and then from his servants in our lives. When we ask for help, we are allowing the Lord to work in both the giver and the receiver.

Let him bless you through others.

Lord, it is difficult for me to admit that I am not able to do it all. I do not like feeling vulnerable to others by asking for their help. Please give me the humility to do so. Amen.

Weariness

He gives strength to the weary
and increases the power of the weak.
Isaiah 40:29

"I just can't do this anymore!" Marie gasped. "I am too tired to fight."

Marie had been battling lupus for fifteen years. She followed her doctor's advice, using preventive measures during the remissions, and she suffered through complex tests and drug therapies whenever the disease flared up. She felt defeated and weary of the whole ordeal.

The nursing staff recognized her weariness as a threat to her health and requested chaplain visits to lift her spirits. I also was able to pray with the chaplain and Marie.

As we held her hands and began praying for her, Marie began to cry. It was as if the Holy Spirit lifted the heavy burden she had been carrying by herself for so long. Her crying was the outward manifestation of God's work in her heart.

When our personal resources are exhausted

and our perseverance and optimism are used up, we become weary. We have carried our burden for too long. We need to relinquish the burden to someone stronger than us, who is able to carry it. God, in his mercy, has provided us with that someone—Jesus.

Jesus said, "Come to me, all you who are weary and burdened, and I will give you rest. Take my yoke upon you and learn from me, for I am gentle and humble in heart, and you will find rest for your souls. For my yoke is easy and my burden is light" (Matt. 11:28–30).

Do you sometimes feel like Marie? Have you been feeling weary as you battle your illness? Ask Jesus to encourage you today, and may his Spirit ease some of the burden that weighs heavy on your mind.

Dear Lord, I give you my heavy burden. Help me experience the easing of my burden. Please replace my weariness with rest. I ask this in Jesus' name. Amen.

Overcoming

In the world you will have trouble. But take
heart! I have overcome the world.

John 16:33

Rob was a Christian who contracted a rare
blood disease. After his diagnosis, he became
very bitter toward God. "I thought God was sup-
posed to protect me! Why did he let this happen?" he angrily asked me (Vincent).

As we talked further it became apparent that
Rob had a distorted theology. He had led a rel-
atively pain-free life up to that point and so he
thought that bad things would never happen to
him. He believed that tragedy should never strike
a true child of God.

Many of us become angry at God when we
face illness. The Lord promised that he would
be with us. However, he did not promise to keep
us from experiencing all the harsh realities of living in a fallen world, including events that try
our faith.

Rob began to feel better as he pondered the

words, "In the world you will have trouble." He came to realize that the Scriptures teach that life will be difficult. He began to focus on the second part of the verse: "Take heart! I have overcome the world."

Are you disillusioned with God? To be disillusioned you must have first been under an illusion. Are you under the illusion that God will protect you from every bad thing this life can bring?

Allow God to help you receive his comfort and good cheer. For although you must face trials, you can rest assured that the trial will not overwhelm you—temporarily or eternally.

Lord, help me accept that you do not exempt your children from suffering. Help me believe that you are with me through this trial. Amen.

Jesus: Name above All Names

All authority in heaven and on earth has been given to me.

Matthew 28:18

Cancer. That word can strike terror in the human heart. For some, there is no greater fear; the threat of developing cancer weighs on them like a thick blanket.

Heart disease. Stroke. These are also frightening words.

We know that cancer, or any other deadly disease, is not the strongest force in this universe. God is stronger and assures the believer that he has power over all things.

When Suzanne was battling her cancer, which eventually went into remission, she learned the power of Jesus' name. Suzanne would constantly say to herself, "Jesus is stronger than cancer. Jesus is stronger than cancer. . . ." She told me that this helped her to keep fighting. It assured her that she had the most powerful force on her side.

She used to imagine Jesus, strong and powerful, walking on her cancer cells and squashing them. This mental discipline helped her have faith that she really could beat her cancer, not because she was strong, but because she had a strong God.

Perhaps you also need to realize that *cancer* is not the last word, no matter how final it or any other disease or condition sounds coming from the lips of an authoritative medical doctor. You have Jesus on your side, and he can give you the strength to fight your illness knowing that he has authority over all things.

Dear Lord, help me realize that you are the strongest force in the universe and that nothing is stronger than you. Give me this confidence as I face my illness. Amen.

Sacrifice of Praise

Let us continually offer to God a sacrifice of praise.

Hebrews 13:15

I (Vincent) tossed in my bed, unable to sleep. My thoughts were filled with dread about the next day's diagnostic test.

The thought of some stranger putting a tube deep into my body and peering inside distressed me. I knew it was in my best interest to have the procedure done, yet I began to wish for an excuse to call it off. Anxiety was beginning to overwhelm me as I heard the clock chime. It was 2:00 A.M., and I was still wide awake.

I began to pray. I seemed to hear the Lord whisper softly, *Praise me even when you don't feel like it.* I felt absolutely no desire to praise him. Still, I did, thanking him for his grace. The more I praised him, the less I worried. *Thank you, Lord; praise you, Jesus; praise your holy name,* I repeated silently, over and over again. Finally, I fell asleep.

Are your circumstances overwhelming you? Try praising Jesus even when you don't feel like it. It will take your mind off your problem and bless you. The psalmist wrote, "But You are holy, who inhabit the praises of Israel" (Ps. 22:3 NKJV). When we praise and worship God there is no room for anxiety and fear. And not only is God honored, but also we ourselves are edified and strengthened.

Perhaps it's time for you to praise the Lord in the midst of your pain and offer him your sacrifice of praise.

I praise you, Lord; I worship you, and I magnify your holy name. Help me praise you even when I don't feel like it. Amen.

Facing Death

Even though I walk
   through the valley of the shadow of death,
I will fear no evil.

                                   Psalm 23:4

Death must come to us all. We may know this in the back of our mind, but when we're ill, suddenly we are forced to face our mortality.

Perhaps you have been diagnosed with a terminal illness and are contemplating the possibility of your illness ending in death. Maybe you are advanced in age and realize that your time on earth is drawing to a close. Whatever situation you may find yourself in, one thing is certain: You are not alone in your mortality. Everyone must face his or her own death eventually. Death spares no one.

The believer in Christ has a blessed hope. We know that death is not the end. Rather, it is a doorway that we pass through to a wondrous life in heaven. There we will dwell in perfect happiness with our beloved family members who died in Christ, all the wonderful saints through the ages, and of course, with Jesus himself. What a beautiful existence it will be!

Often our denial of the inevitability of our death keeps us from preparing for our death. Are you ready to die? Have you finished your mission here on earth? Is there anyone you need to forgive? Tell Jesus that you forgive that person and ask him to bless him or her. Is there anyone that you need to ask forgiveness from? Call or write, asking for his or her forgiveness. Is your house in order financially? Have you made a will?

As my pastor used to say, "We all must be ready to preach, pray, or die at a moment's notice."

Are you ready?

Lord, if my illness will end in death, help me accept this fact and wind up my business here on earth. Help me say good-bye for now to those I love, knowing that we will be together again in heaven. I accept you as my Lord and Savior and ask you to forgive my sins. Amen.

Nourishing Our Bodies

I give you every seed-bearing plant . . . and every tree that has fruit with seed in it. They will be yours for food.

Genesis 1:29

How is your appetite when you are sick? Do your taste buds seem to play tricks on you? Do you have difficulty swallowing or digesting your food? For many people illness makes a chore out of the simple task of eating.

When we are ill our bodies need glucose, protein, vitamins, and minerals for restoration. The amount of each nutrient we need varies according to the diagnosis. Since fresh foods contain high-quality nutrients and are the easiest for our systems to metabolize, they are the best foods to consume. It may not be possible for you to always eat fresh food in the hospital, but you should plan to gradually incorporate these foods into your daily diet after your discharge.

Try starting out the day with fresh fruits. Make a shake of orange juice, ripe banana, and strawberries in the blender. This shake is especially good for those who have difficulty swallowing. My daughter loves fresh cereal made of apples and raw almonds chopped in a food processor, topped with bananas, raisins, maple syrup, and cinnamon.

Fresh vegetables, whole grains, and unprocessed foods are essential to health. Avoid sweets, fatty foods, and processed foods. Read up on the benefits of natural foods and educate yourself about nutrition.

God created our bodies and knows what they need to stay healthy or to recover from illness. He has graciously provided us with a wonderful variety of foods to meet our nutritional needs and please our tastes. Ask him to guide you in feeding your body the way he intended.

Heavenly Father, I pray for your strength and guidance as I make changes in my diet. Help me care for this body you have given me by nourishing it properly. I ask this in Jesus' name. Amen.

The Head of the Body

And he is the head of the body, the church.
Colossians 1:18

Although the brain accounts for only 2 percent of an adult's total body weight, all information necessary to maintain life is processed through it. Any disruption between it and the body can lead to paralysis, other disastrous changes in body function, or death. It truly is the head of the entire human body.

It is obvious to see why our bodies must be intimately and completely connected to our brains. Paul the apostle used the illustration of the head and the body to teach the early believers about the relationship between Christ and his followers.

Christ is the head of the church. When we are intimately connected to him we have significant spiritual life. If we are not, we merely have dry religion. Paul stated, "In him we live and move and have our being" (Acts 17:28). Just as the brain coordinates and controls the activities of the body, so Christ directs the lives of his people.

How do we protect and nurture our connection to Jesus, the Head? We must acknowledge him as Lord. We must humbly remember that he is our source of life and resist the temptation to direct our own lives. We must not put other things or people before our devotion to him. We must learn to trust and rely on his grace and acceptance of us. We must prayerfully read and study the Scriptures.

Are you intimately connected to Jesus, the Head?

Dear Lord, I acknowledge you as Lord, the source of all that I have and all that I am. Help me remember that you are the head, the one I need to let be in control. Help me grow in faith, strengthening the connection between us. Amen.

Confession

Therefore confess your sins to each other and pray for each other so that you may be healed. The prayer of a righteous man is powerful and effective.

James 5:16

James the apostle tells us to confess our sins to each other. Why? Because there is something very healing about verbally confessing our sins to another believer. And when the person we confess to then reminds us of Jesus' forgiveness, we experience a real sense of relief.

We don't need to confess to another person in order for God to forgive us. The Scripture clearly teaches that the mediation of the Lord Jesus is all we need. No, it is not God who is helped through confession. It is the believer who is blessed by hearing the words of God's forgiveness said aloud. There is a certain mystery involved with the act, and we must trust the wisdom of this biblical command.

If you have never felt the grace of God through

confessing your sins to another believer, I encourage you to do so. Perhaps you have a friend or pastor whom you could ask to perform this service for you. After that person hears your confession, ask him or her to say something such as this: "The Lord Jesus Christ forgives your sins, and I declare you forgiven in his name!" I am confident that you will experience the grace that comes from obeying God's Word.

Lord, if you would like to bless me with this grace, help me find another Christian to whom I can confess my sins. Amen.

Healer of My Soul

He restores my soul.
Psalm 23:3

An elder from my church and I (Vincent) were standing in the front of the sanctuary. We were staying after the service to pray for anyone who might request prayer.

A young woman was pushed toward us in a wheelchair. She probably weighed no more than sixty pounds. What was worse than her emaciated physical condition was the look of total fear in her eyes. She was struggling with bone cancer and was in torment, especially emotionally.

The young sufferer was wheeled in front of us. I knelt down to be at her level. I held her emaciated frame and said nothing. She began to cry— slowly, then more strongly, then in long, loud sobs. She felt safe, and the Holy Spirit was touching her, allowing her to express all the fear and grief that she had held in for so long. It came out like a flood. As I held her, her sobs became loud wailing.

I looked in her eyes and felt the Spirit of Christ flow through me to comfort her. I told her not to be afraid, that Jesus was with her, that he would not leave her alone, that he had not abandoned her to the darkness.

Then, after the elder anointed her with oil in the name of Jesus, a miraculous change occurred. The gloom, the fear, the terror, the despair, and the grief left the woman. She became absolutely radiant! Her face lit up, a twinkle came into her eyes, and a broad smile beamed from her face. Such a remarkable change—it was astounding.

As she was wheeled away, praising God, it was obvious that she had been healed emotionally. I later learned that her cancer went into remission for a time. Then the Lord took her home.

Lord, sometimes the way I feel in my heart is worse than the illness in my body. Please heal my soul. Amen.

Solitude, Contemplation, and Prayer

He said to them, "Come with me by yourselves to a quiet place and get some rest."

Mark 6:31

Nature can be used by God to administer healing to the harried soul. Sitting in your own spot by a stream or in the woods or by the ocean can be calming and restful. My (Vincent's) spot for many years was a secluded place in Gladwynne, Pennsylvania. It was a large rock outcrop on a hillside and hung fifty feet above Mill Creek. It was completely isolated.

Through the years I would go there to sit alone. Springtime was particularly beautiful at my spot, but I enjoyed it year-round. During one particularly painful season in my life I spent several hours there each day. It was a refuge from the world, and somehow, in the midst of the serenity of nature, I gained a new perspective on my problems.

There are several reasons why time spent alone in nature can be so healing. The sound of birds, wind, flowing water are naturally sedating to one's frazzled nerves. Also in the stillness of solitude you can hear God saying, "Be still, and know that I am God" (Ps. 46:10).

All week long we hear words—words from people, words from television, words from radio. We need a place where we can escape the sounds of the world and listen to our hearts and to God.

Ask God to lead you to a solitary place—outside or in a quiet room—where you can meet with him often to refresh your soul, to gain perspective on your life, and to just rest.

Lord, help me to find a place where I can just sit and rest in your presence. Please provide a way I can be alone. Help me hear your voice in the silence. Amen.

The Lord's Prayer

Our Father which art in heaven.
Luke 11:2 (KJV)

Do you feel like the only prayer you can offer up is "Help!"? Or worse, do you feel as if you really can't pray at all? The disciples asked Jesus how they should pray, and the Master responded with the now-famous Lord's Prayer (Matt. 6:9–13). Let's look at it together to better understand it.

"Our Father which art in heaven. . . ." Jesus was radical in his declaration that God is a loving father. Jesus even used the term *Abba* (Mark 14:36), a word parallel in meaning to the English *daddy*. Through Jesus, almighty God becomes the loving father who cares about all his children.

"Hallowed be thy name. . . ." Praising and honoring the Father puts us in the right frame of reference: He is the Holy One, awesome in power, might, and righteousness. We are his worshipers, his followers, his children.

"Thy kingdom come. Thy will be done on earth as it is in heaven." This request is a sur-render of the self, of our lives, to the Lord God. We are choosing to submit to him.

"Give us this day our daily bread." God promises to meet all our needs—one day at a time. He meets our physical needs as well as our spiritual needs. We needn't worry, as our God is a caring father who gives all good things to his children. When we think far into the future we may lose the peace he intends for us. As the popular saying claims, "Nothing can happen to me today that God and I can't handle."

"And forgive us our trespasses as we forgive those who trespass against us." In other words, "If you don't forgive others who sin against you, neither will you be forgiven of your sins." If we truly know the grace of being a forgiven sinner, we will know the rightness of forgiving others.

"And lead us not into temptation. . . ." Temp-tation is all around us: temptation to despair, temptation to become bitter, temptation to blame others for our difficulties. What are your areas of temptation? This petition asks God to protect us from what tempts us. The Scripture assures us that God will provide a way out of the temptation. The believer does not have to be overcome by temptation to sin against God, no matter what the temptation is. The Holy Spirit in us is stronger than the temptation.

"But deliver us from evil. . . ." The evil one, or devil, "prowls around like a roaring lion looking for someone to devour" (1 Peter 5:8). He is smarter and more powerful than us humans. God is the only one who can deliver us from the devil's arsenal of evil power. And Paul affirms that we "have been delivered from the kingdom of darkness to the Kingdom of light" (Col. 1:13). The whole world lies in the power of Satan, but the believer in Christ has victory over sin, sickness, and death. In the end, the devil loses, God wins, and his children all receive incorruptible, perfect bodies.

"For thine is the kingdom and the power and the glory forever." This last statement focuses on God and his sovereign power. He truly is in control of his creation and worthy of our trust.

Maybe you've never considered the Lord's Prayer in this light before. Perhaps you would like to begin to pray this prayer, stopping after each line to think about what it means. It can be just the thing to spur you on to deeper prayer communion with your heavenly Father.

Dear Lord, help renew my prayer relationship with you. Thank you for this prayer that you taught your followers. Help me to mine the spiritual richness of it, and may it become a catalyst for a deeper walk with you and a greater sense of your presence in my life. Amen.

Surrender

Going a little farther, he fell to the ground and
prayed that if possible the hour might pass from
him.

Mark 14:35

Do you remember the newscasts several years
ago showing Iraqi soldiers surrendering to the
American forces? They ran out eagerly and
begged to surrender. Compared to their life
under Saddam Hussein, it was a joy for them to
surrender to the Americans. They knew they'd
be well fed and taken care of.

God wants us to surrender to him.

Yet he will not take from us what he prefers us
to give to him. He is not asking for perfection
but rather for us to turn our will to him, to give
ourselves to him completely. He asks us to
acknowledge where our real life is—in him—
and desires us to consecrate our life to his love.

Like the Iraqi soldier, we must realize that surrender really means liberation. When we surrender to God we become liberated from the tyranny

of our self-will and we are freed to follow God's best for us.

When we are ill we can become frustrated because everything seems to be going wrong. Yet if we can let go of our will and surrender to his will, we will be blessed spiritually.

Someone once said, "The problem with '*living sacrifices*' (which we are to be to God) is that we keep crawling off the altar!"

Perhaps God is calling you to "let go and let God." Maybe you need to surrender to his will. Like Jesus' agony in the Garden of Gethsemane, your struggle may be intense. But, like Jesus, you will find that after you surrender, you will receive comfort.

What is God asking you to give up today?

Dear Lord, I surrender all to you. I give up all of my self-will to you. I am tired of wanting my own way. I run to you in surrender. Amen.

Laughter

A cheerful heart is good medicine.
Proverbs 17:22

Is there anyone you know who can make you laugh? This may seem like a silly question, but it really isn't. Proverbs 17:22 may seem like just a pithy saying to some. But there is actually scientific truth to this verse.

Physiologists have discovered that laughter causes changes in the amount and type of chemicals that are produced in the brain. Some of these substances actually strengthen the immune system!

Virginia was a patient I (Amy) once had the privilege of caring for. She was recovering from some serious surgery. What really struck me was her peculiar habit of laughing at just about anything. If there was humor to be found, Virginia discovered it and laughed about it.

She joked about the food. She laughed at herself. She insisted on watching only comedies on the television in her room. For hours at a time she could be heard laughing out loud at corny shows like *Gilligan's Island* and *The Munsters*. It lifted my mood just to check in on her.

I commented on her mirth, and she replied, "I am laughing and for a good reason. My son told me that laughter helps the body get better. So I'm laughing at everything I can because I don't plan on staying ill!"

On discharge day I told her that it looked like her idea worked. As she was leaving I could still hear her joking with her son, who picked her up. Her laughter filled the hallway of the hospital, and I remember thinking, *Now that's some medicine that is really easy to take!*

Dear Lord, I don't feel like laughing. Help me to see some humor somewhere. Help me to laugh again. Amen.

Uncertainty

I will see the goodness of the LORD
in the land of the living.

Psalm 27:13

When Vincent and I were first married we both
felt that the Lord was guiding him to attend seminary. However, after one semester at the local
seminary he became disillusioned with the theo-
logical bent of the school. So we decided to
transfer to a more evangelical seminary.

He researched the possibilities, and then by
faith we moved two thousand miles to a school
in Denver where he had not yet been accepted.
Our ability to earn income was hindered
because I had only a high school diploma and
few marketable skills. My husband had a bach-
elor's degree in youth ministries yet did not
have a job in Denver. There was much uncertainty, circumstantially, yet we were in complete unity about the decision and felt the
Lord's leading.

Making that decision with limited knowledge was difficult. However, it proved to be the best decision we ever made together and produced great blessings for ourselves and others.

Not knowing what will happen in the future puts us in a place of uncertainty. We are often expected to make important decisions without having all the facts. "What is wrong with me?" "Will this treatment work?" "What is going to happen to me?" You have probably already asked these questions, and perhaps you are still waiting for answers. You may have been told, "We just don't know."

We must make the best decisions we can, using God's guidance, and leave the rest to him. We may never have all the information we feel we need about a particular situation, but even in our uncertainty God can show his faithfulness to us. Times of uncertainty give faith the opportunity to grow. Our faith enables us to believe that God will provide for us.

Ask the Lord to give you patience to wait and courage to act in faith when faced with a decision. Allow him to prove himself faithful to meet all your needs according to his great mercy and love.

God's Purpose

Now we see but a poor reflection as in a mirror; then we shall see face to face. Now I know in part; then I shall know fully.

1 Corinthians 13:12

I (Amy) am the eldest of nine children. My parents' extended families lived nearby, and it wasn't unusual to have seventy-five or more people at a family picnic. My parents taught all my brothers and sisters the importance of family values and faith in God.

Dad was a hard worker yet experienced severe financial setbacks in his grocery business. I'll never forget the day the police came to our home and handed me the foreclosure notice on the farm that had been my father's dream property.

The stress that Dad was under culminated in an illness that changed the lives of all of us. He was diagnosed with terminal cancer at age forty-five, and the doctors gave him six months to live.

Only he and my mother will ever truly know what it was like to work so hard to build their life together only to have it dashed by the cancer's cruel spread. Their faith in the goodness of God was surely tested during two long years of trial and sufferings.

When he died at age forty-seven, he left behind eight dependent children, the youngest only two years old. The family was devastated.

It was often hard to believe that the Lord could work this situation for our good. With eyes of faith, however, I caught a glimpse of God's workings.

It was beautiful to see my father's love for Jesus blossom through his trials. He truly became born again through the ordeal. This new-found love for Christ blessed all those who knew him. I watched as Jesus healed his soul by guiding my father to forgive those who had hurt him. He also asked forgiveness from those he knew he'd offended. His heart became softer, and we reconciled our relationship, which had been strained by various conflicts through the years.

Perhaps you also are going through difficult circumstances. Maybe you can't see anything good coming out of your trial. Ask the Lord to help you believe when you cannot see. Anticipate that great day when you will see him face-to-face and fully understand all his purposes.

Dear Lord, I want to have faith, but it is hard to see you through this trial. I do not see the purpose in this suffering. Help me believe in your unending love. Strengthen my faith, and be with me, I pray, in Jesus' name. Amen.

A Sign From the Lord

Therefore the Lord himself will give you a sign:
The virgin will be with child and will give birth to
a son, and will call him Immanuel.

Isaiah 7:14

I (Amy) was filled with grief. No one could give me a good reason why the Lord had allowed my miscarriage. I was told that it was nature's way of ensuring that only a healthy baby would be born. But I wanted *that* baby, whom I had prayed for and loved since before its conception. I had even picked out a name and had felt its sweet spirit. I noticed that most people were uncomfortable when I tried to share my experience with them. So I just stopped talking about it. However, the hole I felt inside would just not be filled.

I began to pray that the Lord would give me some kind of sign that would help me cope and make sense of my loss. I prayed that I might have a comforting dream. I prayed and waited. I became despondent when morning after morning I would wake up with no special dream. The Lord was silent.

About six weeks later I was alone in my car, crying to myself. A song came on the radio, "Immanuel, God with Us," by Amy Grant. I stopped crying and listened intently. The Lord had given me a sign—not the one I wanted, but the one I needed.

His sign to me was Immanuel, Jesus, God who is *with* me. For the first time I saw how he was there with me through everything. I had always believed that since I accepted Jesus into my heart, he resided there. Now that knowledge was changed into the experience of his dwelling there. This experience brought me more comfort and encouragement than any dream could have.

If you have asked the Lord for a sign in the midst of your suffering, do not be discouraged, but be open to whatever sign the Lord has for you.

When King Ahaz was surrounded by his enemies, the Lord told him to ask for a sign to prove he would be delivered. Ahaz declined, but the Lord still gave a sign and told of the coming Immanuel.

The prophesy was to show Ahaz how the Lord would, then and in the future, be with his children and sustain them with his presence. Jesus is the eternal sign that our God lives with us.

Heavenly Father, thank you for loving us enough to give us Jesus, the sign that you are always with us. Amen.

Good News

I bring you good news of great joy . . . a Savior
has been born to you; he is Christ the Lord.
Luke 2:10–11

Have you received some bad news lately?
Hearing the positive results of a diagnostic test
can fill us with fear, discouragement, or anxiety.
We could all use some good news, for a change,
especially when we're ill.

The worst news I (Vincent) ever heard was that
no matter how bad this life may be, it is possible
to suffer even after death. And for all eternity! No
rest after years of toil, rather, unbearable pain and
torment. The possibility of being separated from
God forever in hell is certainly the worst news I
ever contemplated!

God is a God of perfect love and perfect holi-
ness. Our fallen and sinful nature keeps us from
dwelling with a holy God after our death. What
terrible news! What a predicament!

Now for the good news.

God in his perfect love sent his only Son, Jesus, to earth to die for us as a sacrifice for all our sins. Through faith in Jesus, we can have assurance that our sins are forgiven as he empowers us by his Holy Spirit to live lives that are pleasing to him. This salvation is a gift from God. We can't earn it by our own efforts. It is pure grace. Now that's really good news!

Perhaps you would like to receive the gift of forgiveness of your sins. Maybe you have attended church but have never put your full trust in Jesus and his love. Maybe you think you will get to heaven by being a "good" person. If we could get to heaven by being good, Jesus would not have had to die on the cross for our sins. No, our goodness will not be enough to wash away our sin nature. Only the blood of Jesus can do that.

Would you like to give your life to Jesus right now? Or recommit your life to him? All you have to do is pray the following prayer and mean it in your heart. Then forgiveness and eternal life in heaven will be yours. Why don't you turn to Jesus right now and receive some good news for a change?

Dear God, I confess to you my sinfulness. I ask you to forgive me through the blood that your Son Jesus shed for me on the cross. I ask you, Jesus, to come into my life, save me, and become my Lord and my Savior. Fill me with your Holy Spirit and teach me to follow you. Amen.

Spiritual Warfare

For our struggle is not against flesh and blood,
but against the rulers, against the authorities,
against the powers of this dark world and
against the spiritual forces of evil in the
heavenly realms.

Ephesians 6:12

If you are a believer in and follower of Jesus
Christ, then you must face one important fact:
The devil desires to defeat you.

God in his sovereignty allows certain things
into our lives. Sometimes he allows the enemy to
test our faith. Often our illness is a direct attack
from the devil, our adversary. In the Gospel of
Luke the Scripture tells us that a certain woman's
illness had been caused by an evil spirit (Luke
13:11). Other passages in the New Testament
also point to the demonic as a source of sickness.
Not only physical but also emotional illness can
have its root in the demonic.

At the counseling center where I work a white-haired minister comes in once a month to pray with anyone who is spiritually oppressed. He is an ordained minister of the gospel who believes in the power of prayer to deliver Christians suffering from demonically inspired afflictions.

One woman, Leslie, had been suffering severe depression and was not getting any relief from traditional medication therapy. She was a believer and had heard about our special minister. After several hours of deliverance prayer with him, she was completely cured of her severe depression.

We don't really need another person to give us deliverance. The Bible tells us that every believer has authority to use the name of Jesus to cast out evil spirits. Perhaps you would like to pray the following prayer aloud right now. If your illness is not an attack from the devil, then nothing will happen. But if it is, then you will see dramatic results as you pray with faith. Afterward, invite the Holy Spirit to fill you afresh.

Just for Men

He has showed you, O man, what is good.
   And what does the Lord require of you?
To act justly and to love mercy
   and to walk humbly with your God.

                                          Micah 6:8

We men usually exhibit one of two extremes when we're ill. We may take the "John Wayne approach." Remember those classic films starring that great screen legend? John Wayne would take an arrow right through his thigh. He would grimace a bit, then break the arrow right off and keep fighting. Later Doc would have to dig around in the wound to extricate the arrowhead. No anesthetic for rugged John Wayne. Instead he'd take a gulp of whiskey and bite down hard on a bullet while Doc operated. Not a cry of pain was heard from his manly lips.

Or we might take the "Cowardly Lion route."

Remember him? In the *Wizard of Oz* he was the lion that lacked courage. He was constantly complaining. He whined about any little thing that might produce pain. He was a nuisance to those around him who were trying to help him.

We men can really be extreme in our reactions when it comes to facing illness.

The John Wayne approach, while seemingly heroic, can have disastrous consequences for recovery. First, if you don't tell your caregivers what you are feeling, then proper assessment and spotting changes in the course of your illness is impossible. I once knew a man who ignored pain for several months. As a result of this, he eventually suffered a fatal heart attack.

Second, the longer you wait to tell the nurse or doctor how much you hurt, the less effective your pain relief will be. The body responds more readily to pain control the earlier it is administered. Waiting for treatment until the pain becomes intense requires a heavier initial dosage, delays relief, and may cause other, more serious side effects.

Conversely, the cowardly lion approach may also cause serious problems. Anxiety can be contagious. Constant whining and fretting may spread stress to your caregiver. A harried caregiver is a less-than-effective caregiver—something you'll want to avoid!

Ever hear the story "The Boy Who Cried Wolf"? In the story the boy kept crying out that a wolf was coming, when it wasn't. Eventually, when the threat was real, no one paid attention to the boy's cries. Complaining constantly and needlessly can make your caregiver not take you seriously enough when something really is wrong.

We men need to recognize some of these traits that can interfere with our recovery. We need to speak up clearly and communicate our symptoms to our caregivers. We may also need to become less demanding.

How are you treating your caregivers? Are you working with them or against them? Are your attitude and behavior helping or hindering your recovery? Ask the Lord to reveal the answer to you.

Dear Lord, help me to cooperate with my caregivers. Help me not to ignore or hide my pain. Help me not to weary my caregivers with constant criticism or complaints or unreasonable demands. Amen.

Just For Women

Therefore, prepare your minds for action; be self-controlled.

1 Peter 1:13

As a woman and a caregiver I have noticed two common responses women have when faced with illness. We tend toward either perfectionism or passivity.

A perfectionistic response occurs when a woman wants to control the situation. This woman knows what she wants, when she wants it, and how she wants it done. She instructs, corrects, and even commands others to do things her way.

Bella was a perfectionist. She drained her caregivers with constant demands and corrections, insisting that her room, hygiene, and meals be just so. Soon this led to delayed and cold responses from the staff, and frustration and isolation for Bella.

Speaking up for our needs is healthy. However, demanding our own way is not only un-Christlike, it ultimately undermines our ability to be helped.

At the other end of the spectrum I have seen women who take little or no responsibility for decisions about their illness or care. They rely on medical professionals or family members to think for them.

I remember Helen, who suffered with breast cancer. She rarely spoke with staff during her hospital stay. Although she was able, she allowed her husband to make decisions for her. Because she did not communicate her needs or how she was feeling, her husband decided *for* her that pain medication was unnecessary. One evening on rounds I discovered her sweating profusely, her hands clenching the blanket. I asked her what was happening and she said "I'm hurting." After talking with her husband, we gave her pain-relief medication. Helen's passivity caused her unnecessary suffering and her husband unnecessary concern.

As women we need to take responsibility for our desires and needs, keeping a balance between action and rest. The apostle Peter wrote, "prepare your minds for action." We have the God-given abilities and responsibility to think and to make decisions, with his Spirit to guide us. Peter also made the exhortation to "be *self*-controlled" (emphasis mine). We must take control of our own attitudes and behaviors and learn how to let go of control in areas where others can help us.

At which end of the spectrum do you find yourself? Ask the Lord to help you be balanced.

Heavenly Father, reveal to me the way you would have me respond to my illness. Forgive me if I have been overly controlling or passive. By your Spirit, help me discern when to let go of control and when to keep it. Thank you for your peace. Amen.

No Greater Love Than This

They crucified him.
Luke 23:33

The long, thin needle pressed into my (Vincent's) ankle, penetrating deep into the center of the joint. The procedure was necessary to evaluate joint damage due to a bad fall. As I sat on the examination table with the needle in my ankle, tears poured down my face.

The kind nurse smiled sympathetically.

I didn't tell her the real reason for my tears. Seeing my ankle pierced in that manner made me think of Jesus and the terrible agony he endured on the cross for us.

Roman history gives us much information on the cruel form of execution known as crucifixion. We can guess the details of Jesus' death based on this history. After stripping him, Jesus' executioners laid him on the cross, which was flat on the ground. The soldiers found the spot at his wrists where the two arm bones came together near the pulse and the median nerve.

The soldiers placed iron spikes at this spot and hammered through his wrists, deep into the wood of the cross.

The nailing of the ankles together required more precision. The knees had to be bent to enable the condemned to push up for breath. After bending Jesus' knees, the soldiers pounded one long iron spike through his feet. Then about four soldiers lifted up the wooden cross and slid it into a hole. It landed with a horrible jolt.

Physical agony continued as Jesus' body was racked with pain. He struggled to straighten his knees, enabling him to get a breath, only to slump down again. His torture lasted many hours. Death resulted from blood loss, shock, and also from asphyxiation as eventually he became too weak to straighten his knees.

Jesus suffered for you. Reflect on what great love he showed by dying on the cross to forgive you of all your sins. Let that love bless you this day.

Dear Lord, thank you for your love. Draw me close to you and touch my heart with your infinite love. Amen.

The Word of God

The grass withers and the flowers fall,
but the word of our God stands forever.
Isaiah 40:8

Do you know how to use the Word of God to gain victory in your life? Those who do have found a wonderful source of spiritual power and comfort.

When you read God's Word it encourages your faith. Then your faith enables you to endure and overcome your problems. Here are some healing Scriptures that you can use in your illness to encourage yourself. After you read them, say them aloud so you can hear the words audibly. The Scripture teaches that "faith comes from hearing the message, and the message is heard through the word of Christ" (Rom. 10:17).

"Heal me, O LORD, and I will be healed . . . for you are the one I praise" (Jer. 17:14). This Scripture affirms that the source of all healing is God Almighty, whether he uses medicine, doctors, the body's own defenses, or direct miraculous intervention.

"The LORD will sustain him on his sickbed" (Ps. 41:3). This verse declares that God is the source of all the strength we have left in our bodies and that he is close by even though we may feel alone in our illness.

"He was pierced for our transgressions . . . the punishment that brought us peace was upon him, and by his wounds we are healed" (Isa. 53:5). "Praise the LORD, O my soul, and forget not all his benefits—who forgives all your sins and heals all your diseases" (Ps. 103:2–3). These two verses are my favorite healing verses in the Bible. Many times throughout the years they have encouraged me and filled me with hope.

You may want to read these verses aloud every day. I know that as you fill your heart with God's

Word you will be strengthened within and filled with his love.

Dear Lord, help me trust in your Word. Show me the power of your Word as I speak it out loud. Teach me how to encourage myself with it and help me to read my Bible for the inspiration, hope, and instruction that it contains. Amen.

Resurrection Victory

He has risen.
Matthew 28:6

Doreen was a remarkable woman. After many bouts with a deadly disease she seemed to radiate faith and optimism. I (Amy) asked her what her secret was.

"We may get kicked around quite a bit down here on earth," Doreen answered. "That old devil just wants to put sin, sickness, despair, and death itself on us. But he has got some news coming: We win! God's people may get knocked down, but the Lord himself will raise us up. There isn't anything that can truly overcome us. Not even death itself. I'm tired of being afraid. I'm tired of worrying so much. It's time to praise the Lord and stop giving the victory to the devil. Jesus didn't lift me up just so he could let me down!" A big grin spread across her face.

Doreen always maintained the overcoming attitude that believers should have. She had an eternal perspective on life. She viewed life from the perspective of eternity rather than simply understanding things in the here and now.

Because of Jesus' resurrection from death we can all have a victorious attitude. When Jesus was arrested he declared, "This is your hour—when darkness reigns" (Luke 22:53). He knew that evil would have its way for a time. He also knew that his Father was completely in control and that his suffering and death were not the end of the story.

The light of the resurrection is available to all God's children. The victory over sin, sickness, and death is ours. Because Jesus was raised by the power of God, we too shall be raised to be with him in immortality.

Think about this promise. Allow it to lift you above your circumstances. Then you will be able to say with Doreen, "Jesus did not lift me up just so he could let me down!"

Lord, fill me with your resurrection light and hope. Teach me the secret of being a victorious overcomer in Christ. Amen.

Vincent G. Gallagher, M.A., is a full-time professional counselor at Life Counseling Services in suburban Philadelphia. He is also an adjunct professor at Eastern College in St. David's, Pennsylvania. He has served the church in the past as a chaplain and singles pastor. Vincent is a frequent speaker at area churches and is the author of *Three Compulsions That Defeat Most Men.*

Amy P. Gallagher, R.N., B.S.N., is a wife, mother, homemaker, and professional nurse. She practices nursing at Tel Hai Retirement Center, a Christian long-term care facility in Honey Brook, Pennsylvania. She is also a member of the International Nursing Honor Society.

If you would like to share a prayer request
for yourself or someone you love,
write to the authors at:

Life Counseling Services
63 Chestnut Road
Paoli, PA 19301